KNIGHTVI

PRESENTS:

(III)

VISIONS OF TRUTH: "A KING'S FALL[i]"

TC Neville Sr

REVISED, 2019-DEC. TC NEVILLE SR

Inspired by True Events.

You can Share Your Thoughts and Reviews with the Author at:

knightvisions.ink@gmail.com

Amazon.com/author/tcneville

Visions of Truth

A King's Fall from Anointing

TC Neville Sr

REVISED, 2019-DEC. TC NEVILLE SR

Contents

Preface

Introduction

Topic: A King's Fall from Anointing

- The People's King, Saul

a. Who was Saul

b. How long did Saul reign

c. When did Saul commit his first sin

- The Coat Of Pride

a. The seriousness of Pride

b. Self Evaluation to be conducted daily

c. From Pride to Deception

d. Pride and God

- The Coat of Pride and Its Many Pockets

a. What is hidden in Pride's pockets

b. Pride as it compares to James Chapter 3

- Pride Today

a. A leading factor in society

    1. Problem

    2. Evidence

    3. Solution

-

- **Conclusion**

a. **Reflections**

- **Works Cited**

- *A Prayer For Salvation[ii]*

- *The Sinner's Friend[iii]*

- *Prayer For Justice[iv]*

- **About Author**

- **Endnotes**

Revised, 2019-Dec. TC Neville Sr

Preface

"To put on the Coat of Pride is like bathing in gasoline and standing next to an open flame."

TC Neville Sr, 2019

"Many things seem to be new, simply because the past is easily forgotten. The old ways reappear in new guises."

Ecclesiastes 1:10-11[1]

---

[1] Zondervan King James Study Bible Commentary (ZSB Comm. p.1336)

Introduction

Whether Pride today is still the major leading factor (silent killer) in the destruction of mankind, as it were 2000 years ago.

A King's Fall...

The People's King: Saul

Saul was born in 1080 B.C. He was the first King chosen by a sinful people to lead Israel (1 Sam 8)[2]. Saul was anointed by Samuel the Prophet in 1050 B.C. (9:1-10:16). Saul reigned as King for 42 years (13-15). Saul's Kingship failed, and he was rejected as King due to: pride, unbelief, impatience, and deception of his own doings. Saul died in 1010 B.C.. His successor was King David.

---

[2] "...make us a king to judge us. (v.8:5) The elders cite Samuel's age and the misconduct of his sons as a justification or their request for a king. It soon becomes appearent ... that the more basic reason for their request was a desire to be like the surrounding nations - to have a human king as a symbol of national power and unity who would lead them in battle and guarantee their security (see v.20; 10:19; 12:12; see also Introduction: Contents and Themes.) The Zondervan KJV Study Bible Commentary, p.523

The Coat of Pride

"To put on the coat[3] of "Pride[4]" is like bathing in gasoline[5] and standing next to an open flame[6]."[v]

It is very important, whether we be Christians (Spiritual Natured), or Non-Christians (Carnal Natured), to daily check the faucets of our reservoirs (the heart) to ensure that our fluids are indeed water and not gasoline.

The Coat of pride has destroyed many men of old. In this new millennium, although it is hard to identify this new, 'redesigned' piece of clothing, due to its rebranding of the latest fashion wear, we must ask ourselves: 'Can a Tiger really shed its stripes?'

Saul's prideful heart, the Bible reveals, started in

---

[3] A natural outer garment; a covering layer. - to cover with a coat. (Webster's, p.55)

[4] A cause or source of this; Conceit; Arrogance; To Esteem (oneself) for. (Webster's, 223); Conciet; egotism; self importance; self love; self admiration; colloquppitiness: Pride goeth before a fall. (Oxford Thesauraus, p. 1304)

[5] A flammable liquid derived from petroleum... (Webster's, p.116)

[6] Active, blazing combustion. (Webster's, p.106)

Revised, 2019-Dec. TC Neville Sr

Chapter 13, during his two year reign over Israel (13:1-4).

Saul took credit for his own son, Jonathan's kill of the

Philistines' garrison[7].

> (KJV[8]) "And Jonathan smote the garrison of the Philistines that was in Geba, and the Philistines heard of it. And Saul blew the trumpet throughout all the land saying, Let the Hebrews hear. And all Israel heard say that Saul had smitten a garrison of the Philistines (v. 3-4)

Saul made his first biggest mistake against God.

> "When our true motives are exposed, one defense is to become arrogant. Our very pride ought to tell us that our desire to be seen as wise is based on selfishness. Do not boast. (NKJV[9])" (Barton 85)

The Zondervan (KJV) Study Bible (ZSB[10]) list several important insights in the OT and NT, that speaks on God's view of Pride.

1. Ps 31:23 "the proud." Those who refuse to live in humble reliance on the Lord. They arrogantly make their way in the world either as a

---

[7] a military post where troops are stationed (Webster, 116)

[8] King James Version

[9] New King James Version

[10] Zondervan, p. 2665 (Index to Notes: "Pride.")

law to themselves[11] or by relying on false gods[12]. Hence "the proud" is often equivalent to "the wicked." (1095)

2. Ps 101:5 "A pledge to remove from his presence all slanderous and all arrogant persons.[13] "will I cut off."[14] "high look ... proud heart."[15] The arrogant tend to be ruthless[16] and are a law unto themselves."[17] (1200)

3. Prov 11:2 "When pride cometh, then cometh shame." Along with destruction."[18] (1292)

4. "As the Great King on whom all creatures depend, He opposes the "proud," those who rely on their own resources (and/ or the gods they have contrived) to work out their own destiny. These are the ones who ruthlessly wield the power they possess to attain worldly wealth, status and security; who are a law unto themselves and exploit others as they will. In the Psalter, this kind of "pride" is the root of all evil. Those who embrace it, though they may seem to prosper, will be brought down to their death, their final end ... Because God is the Great King, He is the ultimate Executor of justice among men (to avenge oneself is an act of the proud.")" (1052-53[19])

---

[11] see, e.g., v.18; 10:2-11; 73:6; 94:2-7; Deut 8:14; Is 2:17; Ezek 28:2,5; Hos 13:6)

[12] see, Jer 13:9-10

[13] see, v. 8

[14] see, v. 8; 54:5; 94:23.

[15] see vv. 2b-3a and notes; see also, 131:1; Prov 21:4; Is 10:12

[16] see, Is 10:12

[17] see note 31:23

[18] see, 16:18; cf. the humbling of proud Assyria in Is 10:12; cf. also Is 14:13-15

[19] Zondervan, Introduction to Psalms: Theology

The Coat of Pride and Its Many Pockets

We can conclude from the many warnings above that our Holy God hates pride. Moreover, surmise that Saul's pride caused a chain reaction, or gateway (so-to-speak) to additional sin. One of the many, for e.g: "deception." Saul was now a liar[20], that caused serious repercussions that subjected his conscience to doubt and fear.

Saul's further lies and deception reminds us of the book of James Chapter 3, where "Johnson" comments that James:

> *"builds on the OT imagery saying that the tongue must be bridled because it is a wild and dangerous part of the human body, because it can be as destructive as fire[21]. In addition to referring to the tongue, James also says that it is set on fire by hell[22]. James continue to refer to the tongue in negative ways when he calls it a world of evil,[23] a restless evil full of deadly poison[24], and an instrument used for cursing[25]" (Johnson 32-33)*

---

[20] *1 Sam 13:2-4*

[21] see, Ps 5:9; 34:13; 39:1; 52:2; 120:3-4; Pro 10:20, 31; 12:18; 25:15; Jer 9:5, 8 and Mat 12:33-37

[22] *v. 6-7*

[23] *New International Verson; New Revised Standard Version= of iniquity, v.6*

[24] *v. 8*

[25] *v.10*

"Barton" builds on this, and gives us the advise that:

"Christians need to control what they say, and all types of speech, private and public, need to be brought under Christ's control." (73)

Barton also notes the examples of an untamed tongue includes:

"gossip, belittling, cursing, bragging, manipulating, false teaching, exaggerating, complaining, flattering, and lying. ...

[Compare Saul's character above to these examples]

... Before speaking, we should ask, "Is this what I really want to say? Is it true? Is it kind?" (77)

In his book (Barton) quotes Washington Irving:

"A sharp tongue is the only edged tool that grows keener with constant use." (78)

And John Calvin who said:

"This slender portion of flesh contains the whole world of iniquity." (79)

Pride Today

The issue with pride today, is still the major leading factor in the destruction of man, as it were 2000 years ago. Ecclesiastes 1:10-11 confirms this prophetic truth:

"There is nothing new under the sun." (WEB[26])

Most would argue, because they are Christians, read the Bible, and follow God to the letter, it is ok to have (a form of godly) pride in this.

(but left unchecked however, could be disastrous.)

Many would characterize pride to ones feeling towards the number of beautiful things, or the amount of money one may have aquired.

Today, unlike thousands of years ago, we are enveloped within the greatest technological era of gadgets

---

[26] World English Bible

Revised, 2019-Dec. TC Neville Sr

and material things known to man, (clothing, employment type and status', electronics, etc...) everyday it evolves. The only difference back then from today's modernity, was that of a smaller, stone-aged like; analog, economic experience. Nevertheless, pride still existed back then, and today it runs rampant among this new generation.

Let us try to live outside "the box" (the world) for a moment, and peer in and observe things from the perspective of one looking into a crystal ball.

Can you see the things that are terrifying?

Can you see the large showcases of Celebrities[27]?[28]

Do you recall them being broadcast via television daily? Whether, directly or indirectly, what one has, or how much stock or money they are worth etc...?

Lets get real, and ponder this for a moment.

---

[27] A Famous person; Fame (Webster's, p.47)

[28] Hosts, Houses, Cars, Boats or Yatch, to Celebrity flashy churches etc...

There is a line from one of my favorite movies called "The Matrix Reloaded," starring Keanu Reeves as "Neo," to whom was speaking with the so-called "Oracle." The question was asked of the "Oracle" about "The Great DaVinchi," (bad guy in the movie,) who kept captive "The Key Maker."

Neo: "What does he (DaVinchi) want?"

The Oracle: "What does any man with power want, more power."

I personally believe, should one be honest within themselves, that even for a fleeting moment, whether you be a devout Christian or not, we entertain the idea of what it would be like to be someone else (maybe the "Rich and Famous"), or have their living or Celebrity status. I know I've entertained these thoughts as a non-believer, and even after I did know Jesus, these thoughts still poke at my heart today.

I recall now in my present state of situation, (which I hate to admit) that in a sense, I was a "Saul."

Can you recall anyone in your life ever telling you:

"You need to swallow your pride?"

Or saying about you:

"You have too much pride?"

These words for me ran clear in my heart more-so today than before the year 2009 (when I rededicated my life back to Christ)

Was it that, part of the reason people make these comments to us, is because of the lifestyle we are living? (flashy vehicles, the beautiful homes, the perfect job and salary, and so-forth, and so-on, who would complain?) Some would argue, its because those people that make those comments might be "Haters" or "Envious." True as it may be, but we must ask ourselves what are our personal *motives and intents of the heart.*

What about the social media: Facebook, Twitter, Instagram and others. Are we today broadcasting all our flashy status' by posting (and posing) pictures and videos of our houses and cars to various material things? What of the upscaled restaurants we have to constantly update the media that we visited; exotic trips taken? (horse-back riding, white water rafting, jet skis on the ocean, trips to the Caribbean Tropics, under water pics and videos with the expensive Olympus (waterproof) Camera ...)

Hmmm. Something to reflect upon.

Are we taking enjoyment and fulfillment (pride) in the mass number of so-called friends or followers we have on social media, even the fullfilment of their "Wows?" ... "Comments about our so-called "successful life," "entertainments," and "mini vacation escapades?"

Did we ever recall a time, or even now today, where

one of our true friends or a family member (someone wise), close to us would comment that we are:

"Putting to much of our business or private life out there on the internet?"

... but we would down play our motives and intents and come up with various justifications? In other words we did'nt listen, just brush them off.

All these things on social media (if we are humbly honest) made us feel like"Kings or Queens" (so-to-speak), does it not? We would invent excuses like:

"I deserve all this attention, because I sure didn't get it when I was younger."

"I was treated as the ugly duckling in the past."

"I was very unpopular."

"Look at Me now. I have all this attention and more. Even commanding the attention of many (women or men) wanting to talk to me and follow me (on social media), "surprisingly some of the very same people who ignored me during my High School or College days."

The list of excuses is much longer. What is Yours?

We realize now, that we are no different from the actual Celebrity Stars out there. In retrospect, we are doing the very same things we see now happening on TV, only at a smaller scale or through a differ source. Looking back we can agree it was basically a competition. We had to keep up with the "Joneses."[29]

We may also make other excuses, that because we might consider ourselves kind and humble, help the helpless, that our so-called pride is justified.

(The Deception)

Can Pride (Oil) and being Humble (Water) be safe to drink when mixed in the same cup?

By having on the coat of pride, our pockets become heavy with lies and deceit. We have to lie and exaggerate our status' to continue the façade.

---

[29] Who get the most tweets or re-tweets, who has the most followers, who has the most friends, who has the most expensive or exotic car or truck, who is best dressed, who has the beauty of all homes etc...

Personally, as a newly renewed Christian, One can now relate to 1 Samuel 13, and its surrounding context.

Application ?

There was a Christian inmate who became convicted in his heart after studying this book of 1st Samuel as it relates to King Saul.[30] He wondered if things would have been different if he had just stayed silent and not try and fight for his innocence on his own, but instead "let go of the wheel and let God handle it."

This inmate tells us, on the basis of what he know now about the issue of "Pride," that if he had to go back and do things over, he still would never have taken a plea deal, but he would have probably used a different tactic and "kept silent"

It seemed that when he challenged the justice system,[31] the Court system in-turn pushed back[32] and punished him

---

[30] 1 Samuel 506 OT, p.23 from JBTS syllabus

[31] *rather than submitting to a manipulating plea deal of confessing to a crime he did not commit, he tells us...*

[32] Myers, "I'm going to do it my way, or no way at all." (p. 265)

when, in the end he lost his trial. [33]

The circumstances with the Christian above brings

back memory to the above quote:

"Because God is the Great King, He is the ultimate Executor of justice among men (to avenge oneself is an act of the "proud." (ZSB 1052-53[34])

One even think about what Jesus did when He went

before the so-called high priest Caiaphas:[35]

(KJV) "And the high priest arose, and said unto Him, Answerest thou nothing ... what is it these witnesses against thee? But Jesus held His peace."

I recall my Mother still reminds me that our

problems in this world is spiritual not physical, and we

---

[33] We learned that the system ended up being harsh on his sentence because he argued for a jury trial to prove his innocence, instead of taking a plea deal all the other Public Defenders were trying to get their clients to accept; instead of investigating their cases; and to which his own lawyer wanted him to take the easy way out and just plea out because his sentence would have been shorter. Examples of "Ineffective Assistance of Counsel"

[34] (id) Introduction to Psalm: Theology

[35] Matt 26:62-63

have to let go of the wheel.[36] Today we must realize that we are still in pride and often want to do things ourselves, because the stigma and stero-type today challenges us to be "independent." From a Spiritual perspective, this is the deception of the devil, who wants us to not rely on our Father in Heaven, which implies using prayer, faith and patience.

If you can relate to the above, we can admit today, that in our pockets are still "Doubt and Unbelief,"[37]

---

[36] Eph 6:12 "For we wrestle not against flesh and blood, but against principalities, against powers, against the rulers of the darkness of this world, against spiritual wickedness in high places."

[37] Myers, Battlefield Of The Mind:-

Conditions of the Mind:

1. When is My Mind Normal (p.65);

2. A Wandering, Wondering Mind (p.67);

3. A Confused Mind (p.75);

4. A Doubtful and Unbelieving Mind (p.83);

5. An Anxious and Worried Mind (p.107);

6. A Judgmental, Critical, and Suspicious Mind (p.121);

7. A Passive Mind (p.137)

"Impatience," "Deception" (to oneself).

It pains my heart to see how easily deceived we are, even as Christians today.

(God please have mercy upon our souls and forgive us of these sins)

Revised, 2019-Dec. TC Neville Sr

Solution

The solution to the problem of "Pride" is to be "Humble" in Spirit and Truth, and to put on "The Mind Of Christ" daily. (Myers 149)

The word "Humble" is mentioned 31 times in the KJV. The quote previously mentioned above also included this snippet:

"The "humble," the "poor and needy," those who acknowledge their dependence on the Lord in all things - these are the ones in whom God delights. Hence the "fear of the Lord" -i.e., humble trust in and obedience to the Lord - is the "beginning" of all wisdom." (1052-53)[38]

Proverbs, previously mentioned above concludes:

(ZSB) Proverbs 11:2 "When pride cometh, then cometh shame: But with "the lowly is wisdom." (along with honor)[39]"before honour is humility."[40] Wisdom also comes with humility."[41] (1292, 1302)

---

[38] Ps 111:10 "Introduction to Psalm: Theology"

[39] See 15:33: "fear the Lord" See note on 1:7

[40] See 22:24; 25:6-7; Matt 23:12; Luk 14:11; 18:14; 1 Pet 5:6

[41] 11:2; 13:10

Revised, 2019-Dec. TC Neville Sr

Conclusion

Pride is never good, no matter what side of the fence you are on, whether rich or poor, Christian or not. God makes it very clear that He hates the sin of Pride.

Saul's life examples the many destructions that followed his pride. People today are still wearing Saul's coat with deep pockets filled with unhatched consequences waiting to be born.

Pride (as in some of our current demise) can also create enemies against us, or can cause people to become so envious, and covetous to one's status and material things.[42][43]

BEWARE!

---

[42] (ZSB) p. 2346-47, cf. notes: 1 Cor 8:7-13 ... sometimes we can aslo cause the weaker Christians to sin because of our lifestyles and actions that maybe secular or ungodly

[43] (Your enemies would do what-ever they can to see you fail, by spreading false rumors, defamation of your character, even accumulate false witness' against you to destroy you, among other things.)

Therefore, let us be reminded, we must daily check our hearts to ensure that our thoughts, intents, and motives are indeed pure and Godly. If we find they are not, we must repent and humble ourselves before God on our knees immediately without delay.

The longer we wait, we can be sure to see the outcome aproaching on the horizon of Saul's demise as King.

Do not fall subject to the "Mighty Hand of God" to humble you. It is never a good thing.

Peace, Blessings, Godly Wisdom and Discernment be unto you, in Jesus' name, Amen.

Works Cited

Barton, Bruce B, Dr. Min., et.al. "Life Application Bible Commentary: James,"
Copyright by Livingstone Corp., Tyndale Pub. Inc. Wheaton, Illinois
(pp.73-83)

Johnson, Earl S Jr., "Basic Bible Commentary: James - Jude: vol. 28," Copyright
1988 by Graded Press. Abington Press 201 english Ave. South
Nashville TN 37203 (pp.31-34)

Myers, Joyce "Battlefield Of The Mind," Copyright 1995 by Joyce Myers, POB
655 Fenton Missouri 63026[44]

"Oxford Thesaurus- An A - Z Dictionary of Synonyms, PDF" [45]

"World English Bible Complete, PDF," [46]

"Webster's New Pocket Dictionary," Copyright 2007, 2005 by Houghton Mifflin
Harcourt Pub. Company. 222 Berkley Street Boston MA 02116[47]

"Zondervan King James Study Bible," [with Commentary] Copyright 2002 by
Zondervan. Grand Rapids Michigan 49530 USA[48]

---

[44] pp. see footnotes

[45] (Author and Pub. Unknown.)

[46] (Author/Pub. Unknown.)

[47] pp. see footnotes

[48] pp. see footnotes

A Prayer For Salvation

Believe on the Lord Jesus and you will be saved

Acts 16:3

I believe Jesus suffered the Judgment of God for my sin, while on the cross at Calvary. He died in the condemnation that was mine. Romans 5:6-9

I have put my hope in the Lord Jesus, through the power of His shed blood. Acts 20:28

I believe Jesus rose from the dead as prophesied in Scripture, and attest to by many Witnesses.

Psalm 45:15; 1 Corinthians 15:4-8

My hope is in the completed work of the Lord Jesus alone, as the Spirit of God creates His new life in me.

2 Corinthians 3:17

I believe the Scriptures, which show me that Jesus is now my Saviour, Advocate and Friend.

Titus 2:13; 1 John 2:1; John 15:15

I HAVE BELIEVED

on this:

(   )Day, of the Month of: (   ) in the Year (   )

Amen.

Revised, 2019-Dec. TC Neville Sr

THE SINNER'S FRIEND

OH GOD, THY WAYS JESUS MADE CLEAR,

BUT ARE SEEN BY FEW, THY MERCY, GRACE AND TRUTH WE
HAVE NOT DESIRED.

THY LOVE, IS HIGHER THAN DARK HEARTS COULD KNOW.

JESUS, THE SINNER'S FRIEND

PURPOSES OF GOD ARE SEEN IN THE SON OF HIS AFFECTION.

HE WAS DESPISED BY MAN, AS FURY DISPLAYED ITS WORK,

THE WORLD BROUGHT FORTH JUDGMENT, ITS PENALTY FULL,

UPON THE LAMB OF GOD.

JESUS, THE SINNER'S FRIEND

KINDLY INTENTIONS OF GOD, DECLARED, IN THE SON OF MAN
FALSE WITNESSES FOUND. HE WAS TAKEN TO PILATE'S
HALL, HOW LOW HE WAS BROUGHT, IN JUDGMENT,
THE CROSS, AND THE GRAVE, SO HE COULD BE,

JESUS, THE SINNER'S FRIEND.

THE FATHER'S LOVE CONCEALED, IN THE SON OF GOD
REVEALED, MAN'S UN-RIGHTEOUSNESS EXPOSED, IN THE
SPILLING OF HIS BLOOD.

LOVE REJECTED, THE SENTENCE DONE, THE LAW FULFILLED.

HIS ALL WAS GIVEN TO SET US FREE.

JESUS, THE SINNER'S FRIEND.

REVISED, 2019-DEC. TC NEVILLE SR

The Father's love was strange to me, as I listened to the Saviour's plea.

His crown was real, from His thorns came blood and pain.

Sitting there at His feet, revealed my life was vain.

Jesus, the sinner's friend

The Father's light seemed obscured, but was revealed in Him as pure.

Saviour, Friend who died for me.

My heart was black, it did not care, till Jesus, the Day Star shinned His Light on me, and then I could see,

Jesus, the sinner's friend.

D. Neely, Aug. 2002

PRAYERS FOR JUSTICE

LORD I CRY OUT FOR YOUR JUSTICE FOR THE OPPRESSED, DEFENSE OF THE FATHERLESS AND THE WIDOW. ISA *1:17*

GOD, I KNOW THAT YOU SEE TROUBLE AND GRIEF; THAT YOU DESIRE TO TAKE IN HAND. A VICTIM OF INJUSTICE COMMITS HIMSELF TO YOU, FOR YOU ARE A HELPER OF THE FATHERLESS. PS *10:14*

YOU HEAR, LORD THE DESIRE OF THE AFFLICTED; YOU ENCOURAGE THEM AND LISTEN TO THEIR CRY, DEFENDING THE FATHERLESS AND THE OPPRESSED, IN ORDER THAT MAN, WHO IS ON THE EARTH, MAY TERRIFY NO MORE. PS *10:17-18*

I AGREE GOD, THAT YOUR THRONE WILL LAST FOREVER AND EVER; THAT A SCEPTOR OF JUSTICE WILL BE THE SCEPTOR OF YOUR KINGDOM. PS *45:6-7*

FATHER, EQUIP ME TO BE KIND TO THE NEEDY AND THUS HONOR YOU. PVB *14:31*

THANK YOU LORD, THAT YOU LOVE JUSTICE AND RIGHTEOUSNESS; THAT THE EARTH IS FULL OF YOUR UNFAILING LOVE. PS *33:5*

I WILL SING OF YOUR LOVE AND JUSTICE; TO YOU LORD, I WILL SING PRAISE. PS *101:1*

FATHER I ASK THAT YOU WOULD SECURE JUSTICE FOR THE POOR AND UPHOLD THE CAUSE OF THE NEEDY. PS *140:12*

THANK YOU GOD, FOR YOUR SON, JESUS, WHO CAME TO PROCLAIM JUSTICE TO THE NATIONS. MT *12:18*

MAY WE BE A PEOPLE WHO ADMINISTER TRUE JUSTICE, SHOW MERCY AND COMPASSION TO ONE ANOTHER, AND DO NOT OPPRESS THE WIDOW, THE FATHERLESS, THE ALIEN OR THE POOR. ZECH 7:8-10

LORD PREPARE ME FOR THE FAST TO LOOSE CHAINS INJUSTICE AND UNTIE THE CORDS OF THE YOKE, TO SET THE OPPRESSED FREE AND BREAK EVERY YOKE. ISA 58:6

HELP ME GOD TO RESPOND TO YOUR CALL TO ACT JUSTLY, TO LOVE MERCY, AND TO WALK HUMBLY WITH YOU. MIC 6:8

I PRAY FOR YOUR JUSTICE TO ROLL ON LIKE A RIVER AND YOUR RIGHTEOUSNESS LIKE A NEVER-ENDING STREAM. AMOS 5:24

FATHER, THANK YOU THAT WE ARE BETROTHED FOREVER, THAT YOU HAVE BETROTHED ME IN YOUR RIGHTEOUSNESS AND JUSTICE, IN LOVE AND COMPASSION. HOS 2:19

YOU ARE JEHOVAH-SHAPHAT, THE LORD WHO JUDGES DISPUTES. JUDGES 11:27

MAY YOUR JUSTICE BECOME A LIGHT TO ALL THE NATIONS, ACCORDING TO YOUR WORD. ISA 51:4

A PRODUCT OF FAITH SEEDS MINISTRIES

PO BOX 631, MILFORD, MA 01757

REVISED, 2019-DEC. TC NEVILLE SR

"ART IS POETRY AND MUSIC. MUSIC IS POETRY AND ART."

TC NEVILLE SR, 2017

THE AUTHOR, TC NEVILLE SR, A NEW PUBLIC AND HUMBLE ARTISTS OF 2019, VISIONS TO ONE DAY SPREAD HIS INSPIRATIONS AND WORK THROUGH OUT THE WORLD. HIS PURPOSE IS TO INSPIRE AND HELP PEOPLE, IN MIND, SOUL, AND SPIRIT. ALREADY PUBLISHED SEVERAL BOOKS IN PAPERBACK AND EBOOK FORMAT, UNDER #KNIGHTVISIONS.INK:

VISIONS OF POETRY (BOOK I & IV)

"POETICKNIGHT" & "THORNS & ROSES"(A NELLY NOVEL)

&

VISIONS OF TRUTH (BOOK II & III)

"DREAM REVELATION & INSPIRATION" & "A KING'S FALL," ...

HE IS A COMBAT VETERAN, WITH BA IN THEOLOGY.

SHARE YOUR QUESTIONS, THOUGHTS, AND REVIEWS WITH THE AUTHOR:

KNIGHTVISIONS.INK@GMAIL.COM

AMAZON.COM/AUTHOR/TCNEVILLE

ACKNOWLEDGEMENT AND DEDICATION

TO

WWW.JBTSEM.COM[vi]

THANK YOU

Revised, 2019-Dec. TC Neville Sr

ACKNOWLEDGEMENT AND DEDICATION

TO

MY MOTHER,[vii] CHILDREN,[viii]AND MY

SIBLINGS,[ix]NIECES AND NEPHEWS.

LOVE ALWAYS:

YOUR SON, FATHER, BIG BROTHER, AND UNCLE.

"MAY GOD ALWAYS BLESS AND KEEP YOU

PROTECTED IN HIS ARMS, IN JESUS' NAME

AMEN."[49]

---

[49] Numbers 6:24-27

REVISED, 2019-DEC. TC NEVILLE SR

ⁱ Original Paper written on: 07-07-2019

ⁱⁱ www.searchoutthescriptures.com

ⁱⁱⁱ By: D. Neely - Aug 2002

^{iv} A Product Of Faith Seeds Ministries

^v TC Neville Sr, 2019

^{vi} Professor Malone

^{vii} D.D.

^{viii} Alee, Curtis, and Nehemiah

^{ix} Ty, Nicholas, José, and Selena

Made in the USA
Columbia, SC
29 December 2019